W9-AUK-719

Berean Community Church
3157 Kenosha Drive NW
Rochester, MN 55901
289-4179 www.bereancc.org

To:

_____

From:

_____

Children are a heritage

of the LORD.

Psalm 127:3 KJV

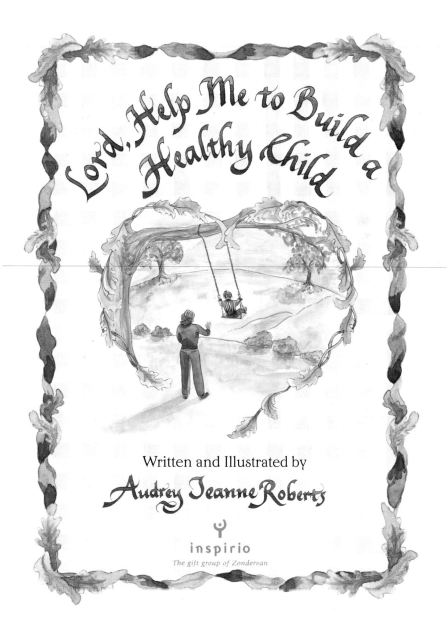

Lord, Help Me to Build a Healthy Child

Written and Illustrated by

Audrey Jeanne Roberts

inspirio

The gift group of Zondervan

Dear Friend,

Am I the perfect Mom with the perfect children? Do I have a degree in Child Psychology? Am I an expert in child rearing? Hardly! I'm "just a mom." I can honestly say I knew virtually nothing at the beginning of my parenting adventure. I did, however, desperately desire to be the best mother I could be.

When my firstborn child, Jennifer was still in my womb, I was filled with fear and concern. How could I ever know enough to teach this child what she would need to know to thrive in life? As I poured my heart out to the Lord, his still small voice spoke, "You can ask ME. I will teach you." That thought sparked a light of hope in my heart and I prayed right there, "Lord, help me to be a good parent. Help me build emotionally and spiritually healthy children."

"Lord help me . . ." became my constant prayer. "Help me to discipline effectively. Help me to teach my children about your love. Help me to be patient and kind." The

Lord led me to great teachers like Dr. James Dobson, Dennis and Barbara Rainey and many others. Their radio broadcasts, books and tapes helped me to learn and grow, but most importantly they taught me about the importance of prayer.

During the next two decades the Lord taught me many lessons and now I have the wonderful privilege of sharing some of them with you. I'd like to encourage you that no matter how inadequate you feel, the Lord can make you into the parent you have the passion to be.

Come and join me, sharing the journey through the seasons of parenthood. Share with me the struggles, fears, and failures along the way. Savor some of the joyful victories the Lord has brought us through. Let's learn together as God answers our prayer: "Lord, help me to build a healthy child."

Yours truly,

Audrey Jeanne Roberts

Oak Haven Orchards
Valley Center, California

$\mathcal{M}$y deepest thanks to my daughters Jennifer and Jacqui who allowed me to share some very intimate stories from our lives in these pages. Were it not for you, I'd have very little to say on the subject of children! We've learned together as I bumbled and prayed my way through raising you two and I'm so blessed to call you my children!

Thanks also to my step-children, Scot and Ariane, who have allowed me to love them and be a part of their lives though they were fully grown when I entered the picture. They accepted me from the start and have brought incredible joy to my heart.

My thanks to my husband Stephen who has taught me so much about diligence and is a true partner in the art of parenting. I never realized how much the kids got past me until you were there to catch them!

Thanks to my special friends and agents Andy Hyde and Debbie Bush who challenge me daily to become all God desires me to be and to grow in the gifts he has given me. Also, thanks to my incredible team at Zondervan: Caroline Blauwkamp, Londa Alderink, Amy Langeler, Molly Detweiler, Lisa Eary, Brian Scharp and the many others who play a role behind the scenes.

Thanks go to my parents and stepparents Joe and Carol Rogers and Keith and Elizabeth Flint who have loved me and encouraged me with all that is within them and most importantly gave me a foundation in the faith that has served me well in life.

My greatest thanks are reserved for the Lord, who taught me how much he loved me as his own precious child.

We love because God first loved us.
1 John 4:19

Table of Contents

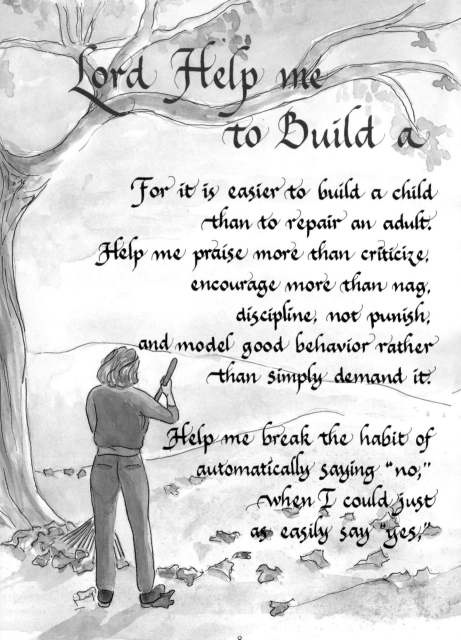

Lord Help me
to Build a

For it is easier to build a child
than to repair an adult.
Help me praise more than criticize,
encourage more than nag,
discipline, not punish,
and model good behavior rather
than simply demand it.

Help me break the habit of
automatically saying "no,"
when I could just
as easily say "yes,"

Healthy Child

And to remember a hug given
before it's asked for
is ten times more valuable!

Help me ask myself
"Will this matter in twenty years?"
then enable me to let go
of those things that won't
so I can have the energy for
those that will.

Help me earn their respect as
I lead a life consistent with
the principles I value.
Lord, give me the courage
to teach them
right from wrong
and help them discover their
own special destinies.

Help me to freely
join in their silliness,
share in their laughter,
delight in their joys and
keep their confidences.

Remind me daily
to draw upon your strength
to heal their wounds and
comfort their sorrows.

Most of all, Lord,
help me really listen for the
hidden thoughts and needs
that often lie behind their requests
and give me the key to their heart
that it may be opened wide
to all life's wonders and possibilities.

Audrey Jeanne Roberts

An Awesome Gift

It was two o'clock in the morning. The house was silent but there was a raging storm outside. I was rocking my two-week-old baby Jennifer in what was beginning to feel like a vain attempt to calm her down and get her back to sleep. To be honest, I wasn't joyfully rocking her with the gentle spirit of contentment I had envisioned for moments like this. I was exhausted and irritated. This first two weeks of parenthood had been incredibly wonderful and equally frustrating.

We had waited three years after our marriage to begin our family. Neither my husband nor I had been particularly fond of children when we were growing up. I rarely babysat as a teenager, and we really had very little idea what to expect. In fact, I was such a rookie that the first time I diapered Jennifer in the hospital, I put the Pampers on backwards!

My husband and I had often talked about whether the baby would be a boy or a girl, as if that were the only distinction. Then when she was born, we discovered that our baby wasn't just a "boy" or a "girl," she was Jennifer. She had a personality all her own. Jennifer was alert, interested in life around her and she quickly wound herself around our hearts.

What a wonderful joy and delight it was to receive this awesome loan from God. Our own baby, a physical, tangible expression of our becoming one flesh. What an overwhelming responsibility it was to consider that this little life depended solely upon us to sustain her. Without our loving care and nurture, she would be helpless.

As I rocked her in the dark, with only lightning flashes for illumination, I found myself pouring my heart out to the Lord.

"Lord, help me to be a good mother," I prayed. "During these last two weeks, I've come to realize how selfish and self-centered I've been all my life. Now my little girl's future depends on my faithfulness. Help me to know what this little girl needs to grow up and become all you want her to be. Show me what to pray for her each day. It seems so overwhelming to consider everything that she will need to know to become an independent adult. I'm scared, Lord. I want to do a great job. Show me where to start."

Lord, help me to be a good mother

The tiniest whisper of a thought came to my mind. "If you pray about one character trait or aspect of her life each day, how many things will you have prayed by the time she leaves home?"

I did the math. By her twenty-first year I would have prayed 7,665 different things for her. Even if I forgot to pray some days and I prayed more than one thing on others, I saw how easy it would be to pray a multitude of prayers for Jennifer. Then the Lord showed me a picture of a beautiful house being built one brick at a time, and he assured me that by being faithful to the tiniest task each day, Jennifer's heart would grow strong and secure over time.

So at only two weeks old, I began praying for Jennifer and her future husband. I thought about the people raising him at that very moment. I prayed that

Jennifer's heart would grow strong

they would have the wisdom of God to raise him well, and that he would come to know and love the Lord with all of his heart. I also asked the Lord to apply every prayer I prayed for Jennifer over the years to his life. This prayer also made me realize in a special way that I was responsible for raising someone else's wife and mother.

The task of praying for the whole of Jennifer's life began to teach me a valuable lesson in perspective. It gave me a growing ability to see past her infancy into her adulthood, and helped teach me to parent with the big picture in mind. I even remember holding Jennifer up to my face and saying to her "My job, Jennifer, is to work myself out of a job! I need to raise you to stand on your own, trust in God for yourself and discern right from wrong, even when I am not there to guide you."

I remember holding Jennifer

As we are approaching Jennifer's twenty-first birthday, I am so relieved to know that prayer has and is still surrounding and empowering her life. When I feel frustrated, or feel that I've failed to teach her all she needs to know, I rest in the knowledge that the God who hears and answers prayers is hard at work in her life. With quiet confidence, I rest in the arms of the Lord and remind him that she is his. And remembering myself that He will not rest until Christ is formed in her.

Our little One

So sweet & kind,
A more precious child
we could not find.
Our joy in you
words cannot describe.
This love that we feel
wells up from inside.

What ever life holds
in store for you.
We'll always stay close
to see you through.

Time flies away quickly
or so it seems...

You're the child of our
Love, the

Child of our dreams

Audrey Jeanne Roberts

17

Jesus said,

"Whoever welcomes one of these little
children in my name welcomes me; and
whoever welcomes me does not welcome
me but the one who sent me."

Mark 9:37

Little children were brought to Jesus for him
to place his hands on them and pray for them. . . . Jesus said,
"Let the little children come to me, and do not hinder them,
for the kingdom of heaven belongs to such as these."

Matthew 19:13–14

Jesus said, "See that you do not look down on one of
these little ones. For I tell you that their angels in
heaven always see the face of my Father in heaven."

Matthew 18:10

Every good and perfect gift is from above,
coming down from the Father of the heavenly
lights, who does not change like
shifting shadows.

James 1:17

Like Holding on to the Wind

"They grow too fast. Treasure every moment with your children. Before you know it they'll be grown and gone." What parents haven't heard these words a hundred times from friends, neighbors, and relatives as they admire their beautiful baby?

Treasure every moment

I always marveled at how the last three months of the pregnancy seemed to go by in ultra-slow motion, and the first three months of parenthood flew by in the wink of an eye! Because I'm naturally forgetful about past events, I often wondered, "How could I capture the essence of these priceless moments forever in my heart and mind?"

I discovered that being able to recall those moments is a skill that can be acquired even by the most forgetful of us. How? It's really simple—slow down. Take a moment to think about the events of the day and cultivate a thankful, grateful heart. My favorite way to capture memories is to take a moment to journal my thoughts at the end of the day. Years later when I read about an event that I took the time to record, the images easily come flooding back to my mind.

You can write either in your own journal or a special keepsake journal for your child. Record your prayers, your thoughts, and the incredible emotions that stir in your heart for this priceless gift from God. You will be so thankful that you did in the years ahead, and your children will know how special they were to you as well. I have also discovered that the simple act of writing events down is often enough to give them permanence in my memory.

When our babies were small, I noticed that many of my contemporaries were in such a hurry for their children to grow up. "I can't wait until she's crawling," they would say. "I can't wait until he's walking . . . talking . . . in school." They were always anticipating some future goal, and as a result, often seemed to overlook the blessings of that day.

Many times I found myself saying, "If only I could freeze you for a while and just enjoy this age." Each age of development and stage of life held such wonder and surprise. Talking produced questions, walking produced intense curiosity about the world around my children, reading opened their imaginations to the wonder of the universe. But time slowly stole away *Change is inevitable* a treasured season of life I knew could never be repeated.

Change is inevitable. Sometimes we anticipate it with gladness, but often it feels like an enemy bent on stealing our joy. Children change so quickly that keeping the memories of them fresh in our minds is like trying to hold on to the wind.

The last time I remember saying, "I wish I could freeze her at this age" was the summer before my youngest daughter, Jacqui's, thirteenth birthday. We had just moved into our new home, a one-hundred-and-twenty-year-old farmhouse located on five acres. The yard had beautiful but wildly overgrown gardens that we were working together to reclaim. Jacqui was curious about every living thing in the garden. She tagged along with me and was usually a cheerful helper. She hadn't made many new friends yet, so I had the privilege of being her best friend for a season. We talked about everything in her life. Those wonderful afternoons flew by with a romantic, dream-like quality to them.

Forget the housecleaning

Then out of nowhere, Jacqui changed! Less than one month after wishing I could freeze time, I had to confess to my husband, "I'm not sure that child is going to live to be thirteen!" It seemed like someone had stolen away my angel and left me with a back-talking, knows-it-all bundle of raging teenage hormones!

Enjoy this day. Don't get caught in a rushing, frantic pace. Play on the floor. Forget the housecleaning and go to the beach or the park. Make memories! Bake cookies, throw a tea party, let your children be noisy, get dirty. Take a moment to simply enjoy your kids being kids. I can make a promise to you. You will never regret a single moment spent making memories with your children.

Cleaning & Scrubbing

Can wait 'til tomorrow
For babies grow up
We learn to our sorrow

So quiet down cobwebs
Dust go to sleep
I'm rocking my baby
And babies don't keep

Ruth Hulbert Hamilton

23

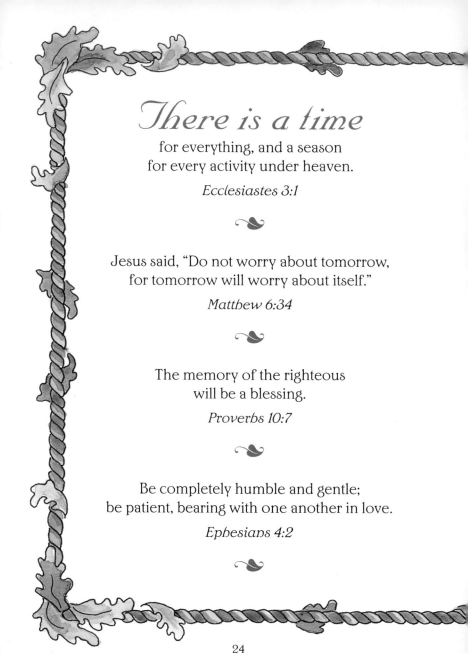

There is a time

for everything, and a season
for every activity under heaven.

Ecclesiastes 3:1

Jesus said, "Do not worry about tomorrow,
for tomorrow will worry about itself."

Matthew 6:34

The memory of the righteous
will be a blessing.

Proverbs 10:7

Be completely humble and gentle;
be patient, bearing with one another in love.

Ephesians 4:2

[The shepherds] found Mary and Joseph, and the baby, who was lying in the manger. When they had seen him, they spread the word concerning what had been told them about this child, and all who heard it were amazed at what the shepherds said to them. But Mary treasured up all these things and pondered them in her heart.

Luke 2:16–19

Let us not love with words or tongue but with actions and in truth.

1 John 3:18

Catch Your Children Doing Right

We are usually so preoccupied with correcting our children's undesirable behaviors that it sometimes seems as though we have acquired special "parental radar" to seek and destroy those undesirable behaviors. Is this vigilance wrong? No, it's an extremely important part of training our children. But often it can be frustrating and overwhelming to them . . . especially when we don't have the same passion about catching them "doing right!"

"You come home this instant!"

"Jennifer Marie Brennan, you come home right this instant!" I shouted down the street into the crowd of kids who were huddled around my daughter. I had watched out the living room window for almost fifteen minutes, waiting for just the right moment when she would be in the midst of her friends rather than playing alone as she so often did.

She came sheepishly towards me, obviously racking her brain to figure out just what she was being "busted" for. The kids all followed her—anxious to hear what she'd done wrong and to watch whatever punishment was forthcoming. There were whispers muttered behind little hands. One of the girls was even bold enough to ask "So what'd she do wrong? Is she in big trouble?"

"I just came out of your bedroom . . . and it is absolutely spotless! I am soooo proud of you. I didn't even have to remind you to do it. Come here right now and let me give you a great big hug!"

For a moment it all went right over her head as she continued searching for an explanation of what she'd done wrong, not yet realizing she'd been caught "doing right." Then, in an instant, her shoulders came up, her eyes brightened, the frown flew away, and in its place was the most radiant smile! Laughing, she ran up to me and received the biggest bear hug I could give. Then she turned and ran off with her friends to play.

I heard them chattering as they walked away, "Man, I thought you were dead for sure!" and "I wish my Mom would do that to me. I just get yelled at."

At that particular time in Jennifer's life, it seemed like I was constantly correcting her, repeatedly teaching her and re-teaching her. I sensed that she was starting to feel overwhelmed and incapable of pleasing me. I realized that I was in danger of losing her heart, that her spirit was being closed down by my constant correction. It was at this point that the Lord began showing me ways to encourage her.

Notice the small steps

Like most parents, I was waiting for Jennifer to do the whole task perfectly before I complimented her. But the Lord encouraged me to notice the small steps she was taking along the way toward accomplishing the whole task. He taught me to praise the attitude with which she attempted a task or a portion of the task that she did particularly well. It wasn't easy. Like many of us, I didn't grow up receiving a great deal of praise. Not surprisingly, I had a difficult time breaking my habit of critical communication.

Praise can be life-changing!

I asked the Lord to help me notice when Jennifer was doing something right and to help me remember to encourage her at least once a day. When I started to practice encouraging her and verbally praising her, she began to work all the harder to earn more of my praise.

This time, I chose to encourage Jennifer publicly rather than privately. It would have been easier at dinner or at bedtime, but I intentionally chose to reward her behavior publicly because of the lasting impression praise received before others leaves on our hearts. Receiving praise for a good deed or a responsible behavior is wonderful, but that same praise, delivered before an audience of our peers, can be life-changing! Jennifer's esteem in her own eyes, as well as in the eyes of her friends, received a boost that afternoon—one that for her was critically needed in a particularly awkward stage of her life.

Another reason I chose to make such a dramatic scene was because it had taken me nearly a month of watching to catch her "doing it right!" You see, for this particular child a spotlessly clean room was a daunting task. It was almost as difficult as asking her to climb Mt. Everest without a rope, one-handed, and walking backwards.

In fact, even now there are times when we would still like to "catch" Jennifer doing right in this area! Even so, we keep instructing and encouraging her, and whenever possible we catch her "doing right." We've found as parents that a little laughter and humor and a lot of encouragement and praise go much further toward achieving the desired results than the customary badgering and repeated threats.

Pick up Your Room

Can't you just keep it neat?
Take out your laundry,
Wipe off your feet!

Childhood chores wear
Both of us out.
We fuss, we fume,
We grouch and shout.

Forgetting a day will come
(Too soon for me)
When quiet will reign
And peaceful it will be.

Your bed will be made
Your closet always clean.
But my heart will look back,
And of this day dream.

So let's work together to
Accomplish our chores.
Then run, and jump
And explore outdoors.

Let's fully enjoy
The wonder of this day
making special memories
while we laugh & play.

Audrey Jeanne Roberts

An anxious heart

weighs a man down,
but a kind word cheers him up.

Proverbs 12:25

The wise in heart are called discerning,
and pleasant words promote instruction.

Proverbs 16:21

Encourage one another daily.

Hebrews 3:13

Love builds up.

1 Corinthians 8:1

*P*leasant words are a honeycomb,
sweet to the soul and healing
to the bones.

Proverbs 16:24

*L*et us consider
how we may spur
one another on toward
love and good deeds.

Hebrews 10:24

Give Hugs Often

I started my art business when my children were young. My youngest, Jacqui, was two months old and slept in a cradle at my feet while I exhibited at my first craft show. The shows were fun, but they were also filled with deadlines and stress. I would often work as much as I could during the day while caring for the children and then work later, sometimes even all night long.

Many times I would be working diligently, on a roll, with momentum on my side. If only I could keep the girls quiet another half an hour, I'd be finished. Then the whining or the bickering would begin. It seemed that I would get so close to completing my goal only to have them interrupt me, often for hours on end. They were jealous of the attention I was paying to my work, and it made them feel left out and neglected. Of course, being over-

I was overtired and stressed out

tired and stressed out myself, I was in no real shape to be an effective parent, let alone meet their emotional needs.

What had happened? It seemed that because I had put off meeting my daughters' emotional needs for so long, when the dam finally burst, there was absolutely no consoling either of them. Their needs had become incredibly intensified. When I waited too long, one story and a little hug would no longer suffice. It took many stories and many hugs and kisses to meet the insatiable hunger of their hearts for their mommy. Even though I lavished attention on them when they got to this point, it wasn't very satisfying for them. We were all a mess.

Then in response to my desperate pleading, the Lord helped me find simple solution. I was to divide each hour in half. During the first half I was to meet my girls' emotional, physical, or spiritual needs and then use the second half to work on a small portion of my current assignment.

The Lord also encouraged me to hug the girls frequently, on their time and on mine. Jennifer and Jacqui would laugh as Mom demanded a two-minute "hug break," pretending that they really had to be begged to give out their hugs. We'd do "group hugs" and "kissing-all-over-the-face-hugs." In applying the Lord's counsel, I learned a very valuable lesson—a hug given before it's asked for is ten times as valuable!

"Can we read a story?"

Over a period of time, I began to notice something really important. As I met my daughters' needs, *before they realized they were having them*, they became more and more independent. After a while I would ask "Can we read a story now?" and they would say, "No, we want to play dress up together, we can read a story later."

I discovered that by willingly devoting the first fruits of my time to my daughters, their emotional tanks were full rather than running on fumes and I actually got the same or more work done in a day. I was more rested, and I learned the skill of accomplishing tasks a little bit at a time rather than in intense, compulsive bursts of energy which was my natural bent.

I was more rested

Even when the girls were contentedly playing outside for long periods of time, and I found it tempting to leave them there, I would call them inside to read a story *before* they started fighting and got tired of each other. Many of our most treasured moments together came out of those "hug breaks." I would ask them a question when I got through hugging them. "What's your favorite Bible story and why?" "Who would you like to pray for right now?" or maybe "Jacqui, how did you feel when Jennifer wouldn't share her toy with you?" We began to talk more with each other, and I realized that because I had decided in advance this was "their time," I was a more attentive mother. I was no longer just trying to make them contented enough to run back to my work, but was focusing on them and their needs instead.

Now that my children are almost grown, they're usually the ones demanding, "Hey, you walked right by me and didn't give me a hug. I want a hug right this instant!" even in front of their friends. Often, especially when I'm writing, one of my children will ask, "May I hug you? You look like you could use a hug!" Just today, as I sat under the oak trees on our glider editing this chapter, Jacqui curled up next to me and snuggled with me for a half hour. Jennifer also came and interrupted me at least three times to give me a hug and tell me she loved me.

"You look like you could use a hug!"

From those first preventative-maintenance hugs, we began to develop the relationship that we enjoy today—one hug at a time!

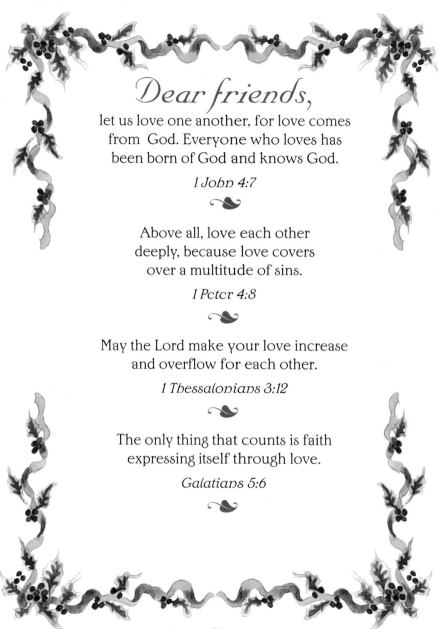

Dear friends,

let us love one another, for love comes
from God. Everyone who loves has
been born of God and knows God.

1 John 4:7

Above all, love each other
deeply, because love covers
over a multitude of sins.

1 Peter 4:8

May the Lord make your love increase
and overflow for each other.

1 Thessalonians 3:12

The only thing that counts is faith
expressing itself through love.

Galatians 5:6

A Wonderful Word

Jacqui was two-and-a-half years old. I watched in amazement as she slowly and meticulously lined her collection of stuffed animals all in a row. With her hands on her hips and a look of great superiority on her face, she raised her voice, pointed her finger at them, and said, "Haven't I told you a thousand times? NO! NO! NO! Don't touch my things!" My heart skipped a beat as I heard the harshness in her tone and the exasperated inflection she managed to communicate in her little voice. Where had she

"Don't touch my things!"

learned that? Where had she heard the words she was mimicking? I was afraid it could only have been from one source—me.

Anyone who's had the opportunity to parent children has discovered what incredibly accurate mirrors they can be of our own behaviors. When I heard Jacqui's emphatic "NO," I began to listen to my own communication and was shocked at how often, how routinely and generally without thought I said no to her.

For example, one day the girls and I were driving around town. I was lost in thought about my day, shopping and errands that I needed to prioritize, and what to fix for dinner. The girls interrupted my train of thought by asking if a friend could come over to play when we got home.

"No" came out of my mouth before I'd even thought about the request. Why had I said no? "No" slipped out just like "Ouch!" would have if I had hit my elbow on the edge of a desk, even if my elbow didn't hurt. Was there a good reason to not allow the girls to play with a friend? Had they disobeyed? Did they have any chores, tasks, or responsibilities to attend to first?

Why had I said no?

The answer to all of these questions was a resounding "No!" I had to face my selfishness and recognize that my only real motivation was a desire for peace and quiet. Let's face it, children are noisy. But is that a good reason to refuse a reasonable request? Of course not! Raising happy, healthy children is a loud and boisterous process where the moments of quiet, peace, and tranquility are few and far between. I apologized to them and relented, confessing that my "no" was a selfish, immediate reaction to my own needs, not theirs.

I thought back to my own childhood and how often I had heard what I felt were unfair, unreasonable "nos." My mother had raised us alone for most of our lives. She was often tired from working and didn't have a second, relief parent to fall back on. I remembered how angry and hurt I had been at times when I didn't feel her "no" was a response that was best for my sister and I.

"No" can be so automatic that it is really hard to overcome the habit! Try to pause a moment and think, "Is there any reason why saying 'yes' to this request isn't the best answer?"

"Yes" is a wonderful word for children

"Yes" is a wonderful word for children, even when it's followed by "buts" like, "Yes, you can pull your sheets off of your bed and make a play fort. But when you're done, you'll need to put your beds back together again" or, "Yes, you can make mudpies in your play kitchen. But first get some old ragged clothes on so it won't matter if you get them stained and dirty." Or, "Yes, you can play out in the rain. But first put on your boots and your raincoat and bring your umbrella. When you get cold and wet, I'll have some hot chocolate waiting for you, and we'll make a fire and read together under the blankets."

Each of these "yes" responses require some extra work on our part, but they are the stuff of which childhood memories are made. Can you remember the afternoons that flew by when you made a fort out of your bunk bed? I can. We entertained ourselves for hours on end (and stayed out of my mother's hair as well!) We made mud pies and cooked dinners of the beans my mother specifically planted for us on the hillside next to our dump-salvaged kitchen set. Mother would inevitably bring us Kool-Aid in our teapot, and we'd have a "tea party" for our friends. It's true that we usually had to strip our clothes off by the back kitchen door and drop them straight in the washing machine. It's also true that when you spill Kool-Aid (especially the red, tropical punch flavors) on your clothes, they will be hopelessly stained. But the joyful memories of childhood far outweigh most of the reasons adults say "no."

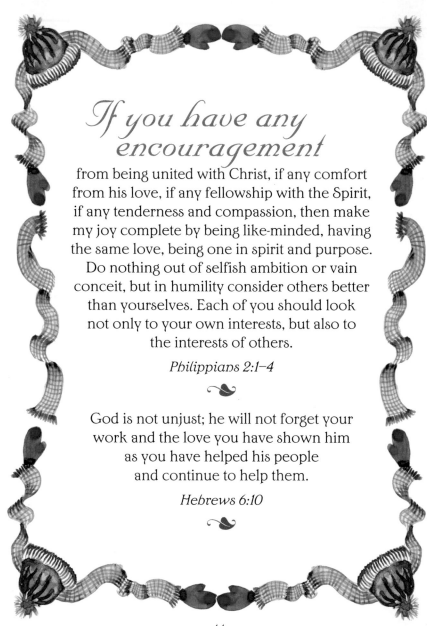

If you have any encouragement

from being united with Christ, if any comfort from his love, if any fellowship with the Spirit, if any tenderness and compassion, then make my joy complete by being like-minded, having the same love, being one in spirit and purpose. Do nothing out of selfish ambition or vain conceit, but in humility consider others better than yourselves. Each of you should look not only to your own interests, but also to the interests of others.

Philippians 2:1–4

God is not unjust; he will not forget your work and the love you have shown him as you have helped his people and continue to help them.

Hebrews 6:10

Childhood is fleeting

like the winter's snow;
take time to make memories
before children grow

Audrey Jeanne Roberts

The Twenty-Year Test

My best friend, Sally, and I were introduced to each other in a tiny church when we were each in the last month of a pregnancy. Her son Michael was born two weeks after my daughter Jennifer. Sally and I learned about prayer, parenting and walking with the Lord together. We would pray on my living room carpet with babies crawling over our backs. She is ten years older than I am, and her daughter Noni was eight years older than Jennifer, so I had the advantage of watching Sally negotiate the "mother-daughter relationship" before me.

One day I was very upset with Jennifer. The specific details are lost. All I remember now is that my daughter had defaced some priceless possession of mine. To comfort me Sally told me a story of her own.

I was very upset with Jennifer

She had a simple, but beautiful gold cross that she always wore. Pulling the cross out, she showed it to me. "Do you see those funny little marks there?" she pointed out some tiny marks that almost looked like part of the decoration. "Those marks were made by Noni's baby teeth. She would incessantly pick up my cross, put it in her mouth, and bite on it. I was so upset at the time I would swat her little fingers and tell her, 'No!' I continually tried to stop her from chewing on it until I finally gave up because she had already 'ruined' my lovely cross. But now, twenty years later which do you think is the greater treasure, the cross or the tiny impressions of my daughter's baby teeth that are permanently inscribed on it?"

I began to think of her counsel as the "Twenty-Year Test" and applied it to every parenting decision I encountered. The test is simple—will this issue matter in twenty years? If so, I need to give it all my attention, focus, and effort— making sure my children learn the right lesson. If it won't matter in twenty years, perhaps

I think of her counsel as the "Twenty-Year test"

I need to let it go. But how can I tell the difference? How will I know for sure what will and won't matter twenty years from now?

Jennifer was now four years old and we were sitting in my pediatrician's office. I was so frustrated that having once been toilet trained, she was now having "accidents" when she was outside playing and frequently wet her bed at night. Her pediatrician helped me to see this very painful and difficult trial with humor and a long-term perspective. "I want to assure you that in all my years as a pediatrician, I've never yet had a young bride-to-be ask me for help to quit wetting her bed. Time alone will resolve this painful problem. In the meantime, don't let Jennifer be damaged by punishing her for what she cannot control. Let her deal with this in a private, dignified manner, and her self-esteem will not be destroyed. But let me warn you from experience that if you make a dramatic issue of this, you will all suffer needless pain."

The doctor counseled us to make Jennifer change her own bed in the morning and put the soiled linens in the laundry room. She didn't spend the night at any friends' homes until she was capable of not embarrassing herself. As surely as he promised, one day the bed-wetting simply stopped! Now that she is getting close to her twenty-first year, we have seen the truth that this problem wouldn't matter in twenty years if we just let it go.

Allow your child to be a child

Relax and allow your child to be a child. Sometimes we as parents overreact to things that are simply common to childhood. When deciding "Will this matter in twenty years," try to imagine your child as an adult. Is it likely that they would still be behaving in this manner then? Would it be a destructive behavior? Then love them enough to help them grow out of it. Enjoy their childhood—it will be gone before you know it and believe it or not it is something you will miss one day!

One Hundred Years From Now

One hundred years from now
It will not matter
What kind of car I drove
What kind of house I lived in
How much money I had in
My bank account
Nor what my clothes looked like
But the world may be
A little better
Because I was important in the
Life of a child

—Margaret Fishback Powers

49

Jesus said,

"Do not worry, saying, 'What shall we eat?' or 'What shall we drink?' or 'What shall we wear?' For . . . your heavenly Father knows that you need them.

But seek first his kingdom

and his righteousness, and all these things will be given to you as well."
Matthew 6:31–33

"*I know the plans
I have for you,*"
declares the LORD, "plans to prosper
you and not to harm you,

*plans to give
you hope*
and a future."
Jeremiah 29:11

Our sons in their youth will be
like well-nurtured plants, and our
daughters will be like pillars
carved to adorn a palace.
Psalm 144:12

Values Worth Teaching

When you consider the Twenty-Year Test, what values are worth the time and effort it often takes to make sure they are instilled? This story is about an incident that I experienced with my younger daughter, Jacqui. The issue we dealt with could ultimately, if left unchecked, have had devastating consequences in her life.

I heard an unfamiliar rustling sound as Jacqui, who was then five years old, came up beside me in our neighborhood Hallmark store. I was focusing on the card I needed to buy for an upcoming birthday, so the sound almost got past me. As Jacqui wandered away down another aisle, that "still small voice" of the Lord impressed upon my heart to follow her.

I looked around the end of the aisle and observed Jacqui pull a shiny piece of candy out **"It's probably just a phase."** of her coat pocket, look over each shoulder, and then hurriedly unwrap the candy and put it in her mouth. She crumpled the wrapper and added it to the growing collection in the other coat pocket.

The argument in my head went something like this. "This isn't just a Hallmark store, this store carries your Audrey Jeanne's Expressions product line, and they know who you are. Do you make this an issue or just pretend you didn't see her? After all, kids her age steal all the time. It's probably just a phase she's going through."

But then I began to apply the Twenty-Year Test to the issue. I knew immediately what I had to do, not for my sake or the store's sake, but for Jacqui's growth and development. I realized that it would matter a great deal in her life if she learned that stealing was a profitable endeavor. She needed *I knew what I had to do* to learn that it was very painful and embarrassing to be caught stealing so it wouldn't be an experience she would want to repeat.

My mind made up, I walked up to her and asked her directly, "What is that I hear in your pockets?" She was in an area very near the register of the store, and I could see the store manager out of the corner of my eye.

"Nothing, Mommy," Jacqui quickly stammered.

"Jacqui, I can hear the wrappers in your pocket, and I know that your pockets were empty when we left home. Is there anything you want to tell me?"

Jacqui's eyes sort of darted around the store like those of a cornered animal seeking a way of escape. It seemed as if she was engaging in a mental tug of war. *Should I tell? Can I get away with it? Does my mother really know, or can I bluff her?* Her shoulders lifted and her eyes met mine in a calm, poised gaze.

"Mommy, my friend gave me this candy and I just forgot to ask you if I could have some of it." She didn't blink and there was a light-hearted tone to her voice. Was I wrong? Did I misread the situation? I took a moment to pray and then remembered it was the nudge of the Lord that had sent me off to follow her in the first place.

"Jacqui, let me see the wrappers," I said. She suddenly began to deflate before my eyes. Her bluff had been called. She handed me the shiny wrappers. I looked them over and saw that they were leftover Easter candy and just happened to perfectly match a display of clearance merchandise not far from where we were standing. I pointed this out to Jacqui and once again gave her the opportunity to tell me the truth.

I prayed for guidance

"I'm sorry, Mommy, I just wanted them so bad," she said. "I didn't even think about it; I just grabbed them. I know it was wrong." Her chin rested on her chest, and I observed knowing eyes all around us in the store, watching how I would handle the situation. Again I prayed for guidance.

"Jacqui, you haven't sinned against me, you sinned

against the Lord and the store owner," I told her. "I appreciate your apology, but I'm not the one you hurt the most by your stealing. You need to apologize to the store manager and ask for her forgiveness. Here's a dollar I'll subtract from your allowance. You need to pay for what you stole."

Slowly, her mind made up, she walked up to the counter and told the manager what she'd done. The manager kept a very serious but gentle attitude during the discussion while she explained what could happen if every little girl decided to take something and not pay for it. Then she graciously accepted Jacqui's money, rang up the

"You need to pay for what you stole."

sale, and then turned and gave me a smile of affirmation.

Today Jacqui is almost fifteen years old. She remembers this occurrence and gave me permission to share it with you. Why? Because she realizes how important it was to her that she was caught and had to deal with the consequences of her behavior. She is beginning to understand the importance of godly values and appreciates that we love her enough to make sure that she learns them while she is in our care.

Not every disagreement we have with our children will matter in twenty years. Most of the time these disagreements are based on differences of taste or opinion, not eternal values. Some of the things that won't matter are strange, ugly fashions which don't appeal to us as parents but are still modest and acceptable; silly, childish behaviors that may embarrass us but are harmless; or music that doesn't appeal to our tastes or sensibilities. Every generation has had to face these kinds of differences.

Some of the eternal values that need to be instilled are communicating with respect; using wholesome, edifying language; developing an attitude of obedience toward God's standards; learning self-control and observing the rules of the household. These are values that will have a great impact on our children's futures. If we learn to discern which issues are worth addressing and which can be safely let go, we'll have more energy available to instill the values that will truly matter in twenty years.

Train a child

in the way he should go, and when
he is old he will not turn from it.

Proverbs 22:6

Love the LORD your God with all your
heart and with all your soul and with all
your strength. These commandments that
I give you today are to be upon your
hearts. Impress them on your children.
Talk about them when you sit at home
and when you walk along the road, when
you lie down and when you get up.

Deuteronomy 6:5–7

Come, my children, listen to me; I will
teach you the fear of the LORD.

Psalm 34:11

Our Family

Kindness We love practicing intentional acts of kindness and self-sacrifice.

EXCELLENCE We strive for excellence — not perfection. A job worth doing, is a job worth doing well.

Gentleness We are careful with those smaller and weaker than ourselves.

Honesty We love the truth and honor our word

Faith We seek to grow in our faith. Walking it out in our daily lives together.

Values

Forgiveness We quickly seek and grant forgiveness to each other.

Patience We hold our tempers and are patient with each other.

Peace We cherish peace between us and all those who share our world.

SELF-CONTROL We learn to control our attitudes and our actions

Love We love because God first loved us and he gave us the wonderful blessing of becoming a loving family.

Audrey Jeanne Roberts

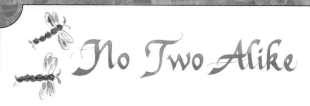

No Two Alike

God made every child as unique as he made each snowflake—there are truly no two exactly alike. Children have so many different character traits, like motivation, creativity, attention span, drive to succeed and willfulness. The list could go on and on! It takes time to learn your child's nature and then to discern how best to discipline, train, and encourage that child to develop into the person God desires him or her to become.

God made every child unique

While every child is different, sometimes those differences create great challenges in his or her successful growth into adulthood. If your child has special needs, like a learning difference, you will have to work extra hard to discover positive, encouraging ways for him or her to learn.

Jennifer was nine years old and I was home schooling her for the second year. It was nearing summer break, and I was at wit's end trying to figure out how to keep her on task. What I didn't know at the time was that both she and I have a learning disability called ADHD, Attention Deficit Hyperactivity Disorder—a huge handle that basically sums up our distractible, forgetful, highly creative, high-energy, disorganized, easy-going, and non-driven natures.

Jennifer is a daydreamer. I would leave her with specific instructions on how to do an assignment, fully assured that she understood what to do, how to do it, and when it was to be completed, only to return fifteen minutes later and discover that she'd only completed one problem! It was easy to get angry and frustrated and I frequently did. I'd tried almost everything I knew and all we were experiencing was greater tension with less and less work being accomplished.

I'd tried standard, reality-based punishments or consequences, sometimes successfully but more often with minimal results. Then I had the idea to start making up really silly consequences for wrong behaviors. For instance, if Jennifer didn't get her assignment done before the timer went off, she had to run around the perimeter of our house five times counting backwards from 100. Or perhaps she'd have to hop on one foot while she sang five choruses of her favorite song.

Energy and giggles were released

For her these consequences were perfect . . . energy and giggles were released. For me they worked equally well because it's really hard to stay angry with your child when she is falling down from laughing too hard. Though I could repeat myself ten times using ordinary instructions and discipline, Jennifer just wouldn't remember. But those silly consequences made it virtually impossible for her to forget.

In fact, Jennifer became so good at remembering the rules that when I violated them and she caught me, she'd make *me do the silly consequence*. I found that she remembered the rules remarkably well when she got to apply them to Mom.

It was important for my husband and me to take the time to learn about Jennifer and to read about her learning differences so that we could maximize our efforts in raising her. There are so many wonderful resources available to parents today. I would encourage you to seek assistance in understanding

God has a wonderful destiny for your child

the uniqueness of your child and of working with his or her character traits rather than against them.

Delight in your child's uniqueness—God does. He made them special and has a wonderful destiny prepared just for them. When you discover ways to help them cope with their differences and difficulties, you may even be used of God to equip them for the life's work he has prepared for them.

Jennifer has decided that she wants to become a teacher. Because of her learning differences, completing her education could have been a tormenting process.

It is still very difficult for her to learn many things, but she has found joy in acquiring and sharing knowledge. Her unique struggles and the individualized strategies we developed to help her cope with them, have also uniquely prepared her to help many other children in the years ahead.

Each personality has its gifts and its challenges. Some are a little harder to deal with, some are easier, but none are perfect. Our job as parents is to teach our children to use their strengths and learn from their weaknesses so that they will become productive and uniquely useful individuals. When we let our children grow according to their own natures and God's principles, we'll be amazed at the uniqueness of the life and destiny he has created for them!

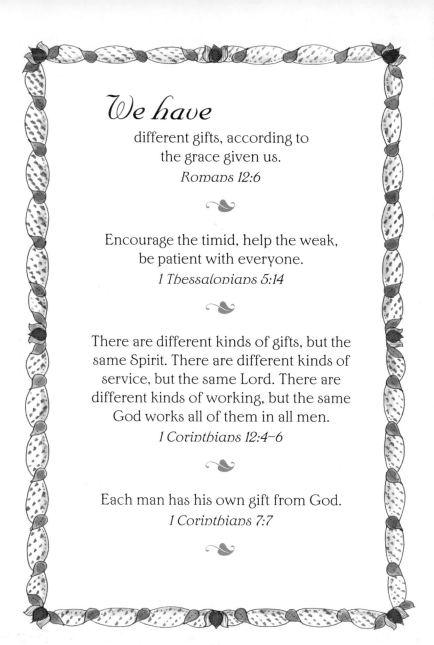

We have

different gifts, according to
the grace given us.
Romans 12:6

Encourage the timid, help the weak,
be patient with everyone.
1 Thessalonians 5:14

There are different kinds of gifts, but the
same Spirit. There are different kinds of
service, but the same Lord. There are
different kinds of working, but the same
God works all of them in all men.
1 Corinthians 12:4–6

Each man has his own gift from God.
1 Corinthians 7:7

Sowing God's Word into Your Child's Heart

We live in an increasingly mobile society. Few people live in a home for more than five or ten years, and only a very few of us are fortunate enough to have families that have stayed in one place for several decades. My maternal grandmother lived in her tiny, two-bedroom home from the day it was built in the early 1950s until the day she died in 1990.

Because of my parent's divorce, my sister, mother, and I lived with grandmother for a little over three years. It was a very difficult time for all of us. My mother was completing her college education in preparation to become a teacher. My grandmother was completing a civil service career and my sister, Brenda, and I were in grade school.

It was a difficult time

One day, we received a written invitation in our mailbox. An older woman down the street was sponsoring a "Good News Bible Club" in her home. A volunteer teacher came to her house once a week and taught us Bible stories and songs and shared the pathway to salvation. My sister and I had been exposed to the Bible our whole lives. We attended church three times a week and were given a thorough training in the Word at home as well. We attended simply because it was something fun to do in the afternoons while we waited for Mom to come home.

Most of the children in our neighborhood came. Unlike my sister and I, few of them had any religious instruction at home. The teaching was very simple, the stories illustrated with a flannel board and a "blank book" of colored pages that facilitated the explanation of the plan of salvation. Many of those neighborhood children made a profession of

She did what she could

faith in that setting. The woman who hosted the study was quiet and somewhat detached from us children. Perhaps she was shy, perhaps she didn't really know how to relate to loud, boisterous, and active children. But she did what she could in opening her home and allowing the seed of God's Word to be sown into our hearts. I often think about her . . . did she wonder if the seed would take root? Did she have the faith to believe that her tiny effort would bear eternal fruit? Did she ever see, with her own eyes, the transforming power of God in the lives of her neighborhood children?

I never had the chance to talk to her again after I had come back to the Lord in my early twenties. By then she had passed away. But my grandmother still lived in the same house (as did the parents of my friends), so I had an incredibly valuable experience in witnessing the long-range benefits of the seeds sown in that neighbor's house.

Each year, almost without fail, a Christian bumper sticker would show up on the back of one of my friends' cars as one by one the Lord called them back to himself. Almost every single child who made a commitment of faith in that simple little Bible study came to a mature faith later in life. They also began to raise their own children in the faith, they sought the Lord for their careers; and who knows what each has been contributing to building God's kingdom?

A tiny seed of faith, offered up to the Lord by an obedient heart, can produce a magnificent harvest. Most of us, as parents, want to see our children nurtured in the faith, but often feel unqualified, overwhelmed, or incapable of accomplishing the task. We see elaborate videos, television shows, or dramatic presentations and think "How can I compete with these things for my child's attention?"

All of the tools that are available today to help you instruct your child are wonderful. They can be used of God to supply the information and structure. But do you realize that you are his very best means to transform your child's heart?

Your children hunger for your time

Your children hunger for your time, your loving attention, and your investment in their lives. They love it when you tell them about the heroes of the faith like David, Noah, Moses, Paul, and Timothy. Each story, each parable, each song and Scripture sows the powerful seed of God's Word deeply into their hearts. These stories may seem small and inconsequential to you. You may feel as though you aren't doing enough. But like our neighborhood Bible study, the Lord will bless that seed and produce a crop that you cannot measure or contain. He is the Lord of the harvest. He gives seed to the sower. If you pray and ask for him to give you the very seed that you need to sow in your child's life, he will give it to you liberally and abundantly in overflowing measure!

Lord,

I want to teach my children about you.

I want to plant your seeds of faith in their lives.

Please show me each day one thing
to share with them,
one thing to teach them,
to read to them,
or pray with them.

Remind me that it isn't great
performances or powerful presentations that
will make the difference in their lives.
It's your Word planted with loving hands
and loving hearts that will.

Please see to it that the seed is planted
deeply in their hearts
and keep them from wandering away
from the Word of truth
as they grow up.

The word

of God is living and active.

Hebrews 4:12

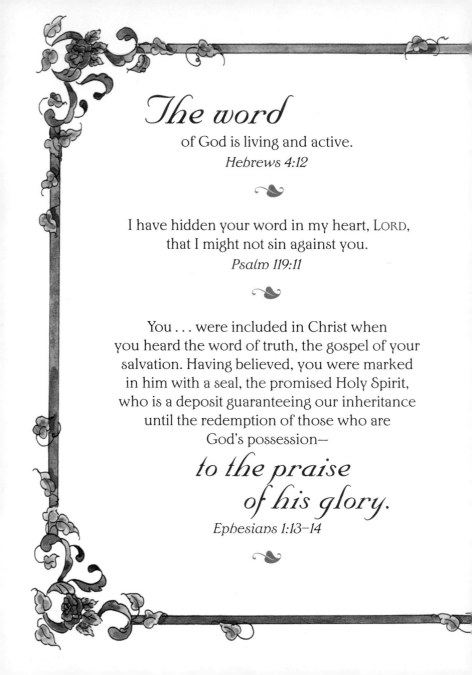

I have hidden your word in my heart, LORD,
that I might not sin against you.

Psalm 119:11

You . . . were included in Christ when
you heard the word of truth, the gospel of your
salvation. Having believed, you were marked
in him with a seal, the promised Holy Spirit,
who is a deposit guaranteeing our inheritance
until the redemption of those who are
God's possession—

to the praise of his glory.

Ephesians 1:13–14

Faith

comes from hearing the message, and the
message is heard through the word of Christ.
Romans 10:17

The one who sows to please the Spirit,
from the Spirit will reap eternal life.
Galatians 6:8

Remember this: Whoever sows sparingly
will also reap sparingly, and whoever sows
generously will also reap generously.
2 Corinthians 9:6

The one who received the seed that fell on
good soil is the man who hears the word and
understands it. He produces a crop, yielding a
hundred, sixty or thirty times what was sown.
Matthew 13:23

Earning Your Child's Respect

I was a rather argumentative young child (to put it mildly). My family would often comment that I argued as a form of entertainment, and my cousin's well-deserved nickname for me was "Ornery."

One afternoon when I was about ten years old, my grandmother was attempting to instruct me to do a particularly disgusting household task.

"It's not fair!" I exclaimed after my grandmother answered

"It's not fair!"

each of my well-reasoned arguments outlining why I shouldn't have to do something she wasn't willing to do.

"Do what I say, not what I do," my grandmother snapped back in utter frustration. This phrase was a rather common one of her generation, and I don't think she even realized the implications of what she was saying. But to my child's heart and acutely sensitive sense of fairness and justice, it seemed like just plain hypocrisy.

Have you noticed how children watch everything we do to see if it matches up with what we're saying? When it does, they develop a wonderful sense of trust and confidence in our leadership. However if it doesn't, all the effort we expend to teach them our values falls on deaf ears and stony hearts.

My Jacqui is a lot like I was as a child. We teased her for years that she was either going to be a lawyer or a salesperson because of her love of arguing the finer points of the law and her inability to take no for an answer! When she was little, I declared more than once that I had no concerns that she would follow anyone into trouble—because if she headed towards trouble she'd be the leader of the pack!

Jacqui tested every authority figure in her life, myself and my husband included. Only when someone proved worthy of respect, would she willingly follow his or her lead. This led to some interesting encounters over the years with teachers, coaches, and even family members. I tried to figure out what the difference was in the way we each handled Jacqui.

I was honest about my own flaws

After praying about it, the Lord showed me that in all of my dealings with Jacqui, I had never required her to live up to a standard I wasn't willing to set as a goal for myself. If I disciplined her for lying, I could honestly ask her, "Have you ever heard me lie to you or intentionally tell you something I knew was wrong?" I was also determined to be honest and vulnerable about my own flaws and frailties with her and had tried to lead her by example.

I found tremendous freedom in not pretending to my children that I was perfect and instead allowed them to observe the process of God changing my heart and convicting me of my own sins and failures. When I was wrong in the way I made a decision or handled a conflict, I would say so and ask for their forgiveness. The result was that they seemed to respect me more, not less. I felt tremendous grace from them, especially in the areas where I was the weakest as a mother. I think that when I was real, they felt safe being real as well.

They seemed to respect me more

You secure your children's respect in subtle ways through the opportunities to walk in integrity that occur every day. For example, you might be standing in line at the movie theatre and the clerk says, "Three adults and one child?" But your child knows she is twelve and counts for an adult ticket. Buying her the more expensive ticket is a small price to pay to be an example of truth and honor. Or when you are expecting a phone call you don't want to take, don't have your child say, "She's not home right now." It is in the littlest daily decisions that our integrity will show the most.

I was afraid when I began raising my children that if we set high moral standards in our home it would lead to the same kinds of arguments and rebellion that I had experienced growing up. The church I was raised in was an old-line denomination that is somewhat legalistic. When I became a teenager, rather than staying in the church and embracing my parent's values, I ran as hard as I could away from them. In retrospect, it seemed that the church clearly and faithfully taught the principles and commandments of God's Word, but they didn't communicate *why God gave us his rules and instructions.*

I returned to the Lord a few years before we started our family, and during those years he began to teach me that it was his deep and abiding love for me that caused him to place restrictions upon my life. He didn't want me to be hurt by making wrong choices. He wanted my life to be rich, happy, and blessed! Coming to that understanding in my own life helped me to teach my children the same thing about God's rules and then subsequently our own family rules.

Along the way my family and I have learned many lessons together. Earning my children's respect has been a

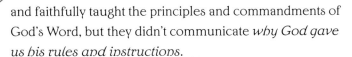

He didn't want me to be hurt

delightful process and has come probably as much from consciously doing the right things as avoiding the wrong ones! I discovered that teaching is best done by example. The old adage "Actions speak louder than words" is surely true. It was much easier for my children to be polite when I modeled politeness for them. They saw the value of holding their tempers when I showed them I could learn to hold mine as well. It became natural for them to be generous with their things when they observed the joy it brought to our family when we gave to those less fortunate, no matter how lean our means. My children more readily forgave after experiencing my forgiveness of them, and they found it much easier to love others after having experienced the blessing of our family's unconditional love for each other.

It has been a joy teaching the principles of godliness to our children. They've seen firsthand that we are happy living under God's rules. They've also had the opportunity to observe the long-term consequences of disobeying God's principles when people around us made poor choices and we've talked about the results of those choices in their lives.

"Do as I say *and as I do*" is a wonderful parental motto. When followed, you can become the best picture of Jesus your children will ever see and be a living example that makes it easy for them to respect and embrace your values.

Time & Love

A child's
Heart
Can't tell
Them
apart

Audrey Jeanne Roberts

*In everything
set them an example
by doing what
is good.*

Titus 2:7

A kindhearted woman
gains respect.
Proverbs 11:16

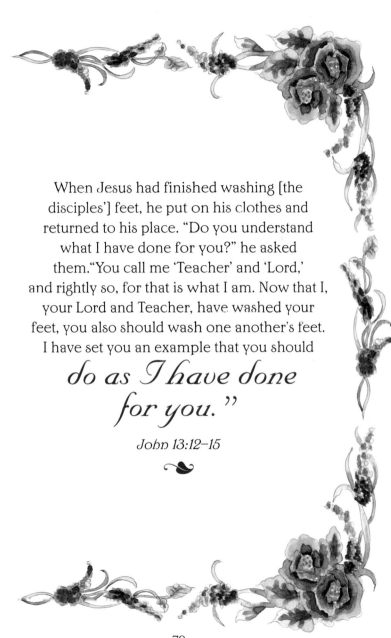

When Jesus had finished washing [the disciples'] feet, he put on his clothes and returned to his place. "Do you understand what I have done for you?" he asked them."You call me 'Teacher' and 'Lord,' and rightly so, for that is what I am. Now that I, your Lord and Teacher, have washed your feet, you also should wash one another's feet. I have set you an example that you should

do as I have done for you."

John 13:12–15

I Love You

I love you enough to say no,
to do the things that are right for you
not just what makes you feel good
for the moment.
I love you enough to meet your needs
to be warm, protected, clothed,
fed and cared for, but above all
to be loved unconditionally.

I love you enough
to have you not like me sometimes.
I want to be your friend,
but more importantly,
I want to be a good parent
and do what is
right for your life.

Enough

I love you enough
to teach you right from wrong.
To train you to make right choices
 and help you grow to become a person
     of character:
kind, loving, thankful, diligent, truthful,
     patient and self-disciplined.

And when my job is done...
I hope one day to hear you say to
your own children,

I love you enough

Audrey Jeanne Roberts

Of Greater Worth Than Gold

There's something about the moment when a priceless treasure is broken that imprints itself upon your mind. My daughter Jennifer was about five. She was at the delightful stage in development where she constantly wanted to be "Mommy's helper."

She wanted to be Mommy's helper

I was returning from visiting my grandmother, who had had a stroke six years earlier. That afternoon, my mother had given me a beautiful, twelve-inch tall, thick crystal vase that Grandmother wanted me to have.

I treasured it, but not because the vase was an antique. In fact I was with Grandmother when she "splurged" on herself and bought it at the military exchange. The vase's great value was derived solely from the heart. When I looked at it, a flood of memories played across my mind's eye.

Arriving home, I grabbed a few items from the side door of the van and headed into the house. Jennifer ran out to greet me with sparkling eyes and arms spread wide.

She wanted to give me all the love her five-year-old heart could express.

I left her on the porch, stepped into the living room and set down my first load. As I stepped out the door, I looked across the front lawn just in time to see Jennifer hit the button to open the back hatch of the van. I didn't have time to shout, "Don't 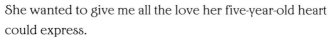 open that door!" Frame by frame, in slow motion, the drama unfolded. To this day I can recall every detail of the next three seconds.

Slowly, the hydraulic lifts raised the door and a flash of rainbow-sparkling light reflected off of the crystal vase as it rolled out the back and broke into a thousand pieces at Jennifer's feet.

In that instant, the moment just before Jennifer realized what she had done, I had a decision to make. Was I going to shatter my little girl's heart just like she had accidentally shattered my priceless treasure?

The gentle voice of the Lord spoke to my heart in that moment. "You have an opportunity to teach her a lesson that will live on in her heart for a lifetime. No matter how you choose to react, the vase will never be anything more than a memory. You need to reassure her that she is worth more to you than a thousand crystal vases."

I couldn't speak. I just ran to Jennifer. She looked up at me, her eyes spilling over with tears and an expression of sheer panic on her face. "Mommy, I didn't mean to! Mommy, I didn't know it was there! Mommy, I'm so sorry!"

I took her in my arms, held her close and said, "Jennifer, that vase was very beautiful. It was special to me because it was special to your great-grandmother. But it can never compare with how valuable you are to me. You weren't careless, or thoughtless . . . it was an accident. Things are

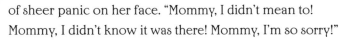

"Mommy, I didn't mean to!"

important and it's important that you know how to care for them. But there isn't anything on this earth . . . not houses or money or jewels or priceless antiques that are more valuable than you are. I know you didn't mean to break that vase and I forgive you. We both wish we could 'rewind the tape,' but the moment has happened and nothing can change it. I love you, Jennifer. It's okay."

In that instant, Jennifer experienced a life-defining moment. She had been terrified that I would be angry at her. She knew that vase was of great worth to me. She was helpless to turn back the clock and undo the wrong. Handled ineffectively she might have been deeply scarred. But by the Lord instructing me to give her grace and under-standing, she came to a deep understanding that things are important, but not as important as people.

Like the Lord promised, this has manifested itself all throughout Jennifer's life. She has remembered the lesson and rests secure that she will be loved no matter what and that she is more important than any material possession.

Communicating to your children how incredibly valuable they are to you is vitally important. Make sure they know that they are more valuable than possessions, position, or wealth—not just by your words, but through your actions as well. Teach them that they are of greater worth than gold. It will be one of the best ways you can create a deep and abiding sense of security in their hearts.

Children...

Some measure riches
in silver & gold.
Of these have we little,
yet treasures untold.
Eyes that sparkle &
smiles that gleam,

laughter, giggles
even tears it seems.
Have brought to us
life's most lasting
pleasures
For our children

are a

priceless treasure

Welcome to my Playhouse

Audrey Jeanne Roberts

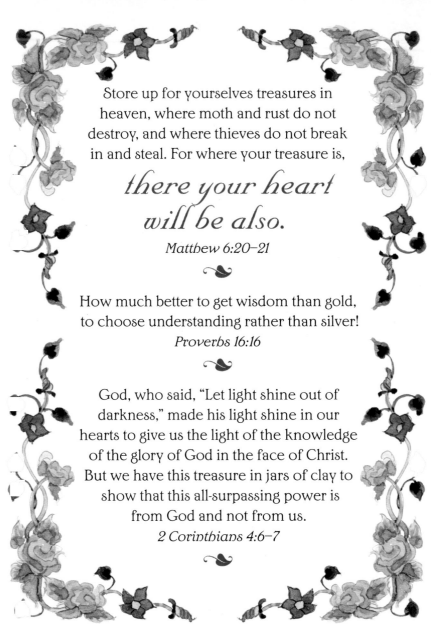

Store up for yourselves treasures in heaven, where moth and rust do not destroy, and where thieves do not break in and steal. For where your treasure is,

there your heart will be also.

Matthew 6:20–21

How much better to get wisdom than gold, to choose understanding rather than silver!

Proverbs 16:16

God, who said, "Let light shine out of darkness," made his light shine in our hearts to give us the light of the knowledge of the glory of God in the face of Christ. But we have this treasure in jars of clay to show that this all-surpassing power is from God and not from us.

2 Corinthians 4:6–7

Invest in Your Children

Children are somewhat like financial investments. While there's no guarantee how much an investment will grow, there is a guarantee that it can't grow if it isn't funded in the first place. Like any financial instrument small, consistent, early investments will yield the greatest rewards.

When we became parents, my husband and I determined I would stay home and raise our children. It was not an easy choice. We had no savings and my husband had just been out of work for sixteen months. It was 1981 and the feminist movement was at its peak. The media and many of our friends and neighbors communicated in subtle and not-so-subtle ways that I was wasting my life and my talents.

Then there were the physical sacrifices. Our cars were old and often unreliable. Our furniture consisted of hand-me-downs and garage sale finds. Our carpets were threadbare. We barely made ends meet. Yet even with all the difficulties we faced in those years, if you asked me now, "Would you make the sacrifices all over again?" I would answer yes without a moment's hesitation.

Our home may not have been the most elegant or fashionable, but the smiles on our children's faces made up for anything we may have lacked. In fact, with the perspective of time I would have let go of more, not less. I would have pursued less of my own interests and shared more of theirs. I would have sought to be more attentive to my children, for I must confess, even as I was physically attending to the routine chores of parenting, often my mind and heart were far, far away.

This morning, I asked my children, "What was the most valuable thing you remember me doing for you as a mother?" Neither Jennifer nor Jacqui mentioned anything we bought them or owned as a family. They didn't mention the kind of house we lived in, car we drove or the clothes they wore. Instead, their answers were identical. "You spent time talking with us. You listened and didn't over-react when we shared our thoughts or experiences. You took the time to become our very best friend. When our father died and life was hard, we knew we could talk to you about everything we were feeling, because we had already been doing it for years."

Hearing them share this was a great affirmation of the value my children placed on the choices I had made in life, because like every parent, I often worry whether I'm doing a good enough job. One afternoon a few years ago, I was being particularly hard on myself, recounting my imperfections as a mother, when Jacqui put her hands on her hips and began lecturing me.

"Now let me see if I have this correct," Jacqui said. "Because you're a mom, you're supposed to be perfect?

What is it you're always telling us? 'Have you given it your best? Have you done all you could and given every effort to do a good job? Then be satisfied with what you were able to accomplish and keep trying to do it better.' You aren't perfect, but you're the perfect mom for me!"

In that moment, no sacrifice I made could have measured up to the sense of joy and accomplishment I felt. For all my failures and imperfections, Jacqui had trusted my heart was right towards her. She knew I cared enough to try with all that was within me to be a good parent. She knew she was loved and that I would do what was best for her. In return, she was willing to give me a lot of grace.

Our earthly bank accounts are still pretty lean. Our cars are still old and less than reliable. Our home is wonderful, but it is neither large nor impressively decorated. Still, we are incredibly rich—rich in memories, rich in love, rich in success where it matters most—our home and family life.

May you be challenged and encouraged to passionately and faithfully pray for your children—for at the end of life, what earthly investment could pay any greater rewards? Make the investment and you too will reap the incredible blessings that will flow out of the heart of your healthy child.

Sow for yourselves righteousness,
    reap the fruit of unfailing love,
and break up your unplowed ground;
    for it is time to seek the Lord,
until he comes
    and showers righteousness on you.
Hosea 10:12

Give, and it will be given to you. A good measure, pressed down, shaken together and running over, will be poured into your lap. For with the measure you use, it will be measured to you.
Luke 6:38

Do not forget to do good
and to share with others, for with such sacrifices God is pleased.
Hebrews 13:16

"As the heavens are higher than the earth,

so are my ways higher than your ways
    and my thoughts than your thoughts.
As the rain and the snow
    come down from heaven,
and do not return to it
    without watering the earth
and making it bud and flourish,
    so that it yields seed for the sower and
        bread for the eater,
so is my word that goes out from my mouth:
    It will not return to me empty,
but will accomplish what I desire
    and achieve the purpose for which I sent it,"
        says the LORD.

Isaiah 55:9–11

My child, when you were conceived
I held you deep inside...
In the circle of my womb.
We were so close,
We shared everything,
you and I.
On the day you were born
I held you in the circle
of my arms
Joyously sharing you
With those I loved
the most.

Then when you seemed to fit
Just right, you began to
walk and talk
And grow and the circle of my arms
Had to open more and more,
Your gangly arms and legs began
Spreading outside of my reach...

...The Circle of Love...

...The Circle of L

My circle could no longer contain
All you were becoming!

Now I watch your life moving
Into even bigger circles,
Uniquely your own...
A tiny part of me fears
I will stand apart.
Alone... somewhere outside
your heart...
But the greater part
of me knows
You will carry with you
The values, wisdom and
truth shared
Within our circle of love.

And now I know, as I walk the path
Of all who have passed this way before,
It's in the letting go that
The circle of love begins again.

Audrey Jeanne Roberts

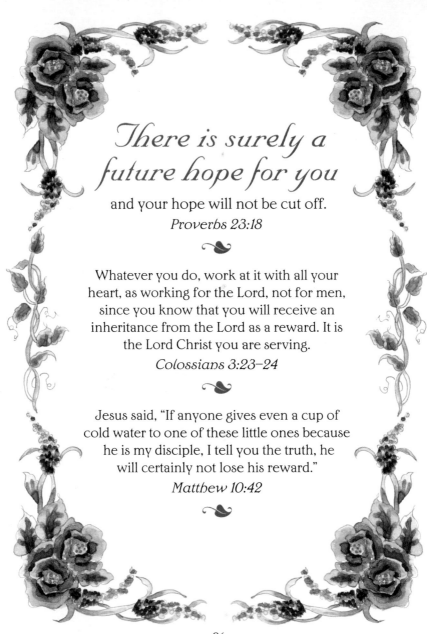

There is surely a future hope for you

and your hope will not be cut off.

Proverbs 23:18

Whatever you do, work at it with all your
heart, as working for the Lord, not for men,
since you know that you will receive an
inheritance from the Lord as a reward. It is
the Lord Christ you are serving.

Colossians 3:23–24

Jesus said, "If anyone gives even a cup of
cold water to one of these little ones because
he is my disciple, I tell you the truth, he
will certainly not lose his reward."

Matthew 10:42